APJ
Abdul Kalam

www.pegasusforkids.com

© B. Jain Publishers (P) Ltd. All rights reserved. No part of this book may be reproduced, stored in a retrieval system or transmitted, in any form or by any means, mechanical, photocopying, recording or otherwise, without any prior written permission of the publisher.

Published by Kuldeep Jain for B. Jain Publishers (P) Ltd., D-157, Sector 63, Noida - 201307, U.P
Registered office: 1921/10, Chuna Mandi, Paharganj, New Delhi-110055

Printed in India

Contents

- 5   Who was Kalam?
- 6   Early Life and Education
- 16   Career as a Scientist
- 32   Personal Life
- 35   Leading the Country
- 39   Post-Presidency
- 42   Final Parting
- 48   Kalam, the Author
- 54   Awards and Accolades
- 57   Timeline
- 59   Activities
- 62   Glossary

Who was Kalam?

Avul Pakir Jainulabdeen Abdul Kalam, better known as A.P.J. Abdul Kalam, was born on October 15, 1931 in Rameswaram, India. He was an Indian scientist and politician who played a key role in the development of India's missile and nuclear weapons programmes. Appointed as the eleventh president of India, Kalam served his term in office from 2002 to 2007. He was elected against Lakshmi Sehgal in 2002 and had support from both the Bharatiya Janata Party and the Indian National Congress—the two leading parties of Indian politics.

Kalam was one of the few presidents who touched the hearts of millions of people and left an indelible imprint on their minds. It is owing to this popularity he enjoyed among the masses that he came to be called People's President. A scientist by profession, he worked with Indian Space Research Organisation (ISRO) and Defense Research and Development Organisation (DRDO) as an aerospace engineer before assuming his role as the president of India. His work on the development of launch vehicle and ballistic missile technology earned him the name 'Missile Man of India'.

Early Life and Education

Abdul Kalam was born on October 15, 1931 into a Tamil Muslim family in the pilgrimage centre of Rameswaram on Pamban Island, then in the Madras Presidency and now in the State of Tamil Nadu. His father, Jainulabudeen, was a boat owner and imam of a local mosque. His mother, Ashiamma, was a home-maker. His father owned a ferry that took Hindu pilgrims back and forth between Rameswaram and the now uninhabited Dhanushkodi.

In his family, Kalam was the youngest of four brothers and one sister in his family. His ancestors had been wealthy traders and landowners, with numerous properties and large tracts of land. Their business involved trading groceries between the mainland and the island and to and from Sri Lanka, as well as ferrying pilgrims between the mainland and Pamban. With the opening of the Pamban Bridge to the mainland in 1914, their businesses failed and the family fortune and properties were lost over time, apart from the ancestral home. By his early childhood, Kalam's family was struggling to make ends meet. Hence, Kalam, from an early age, took to selling newspapers to supplement his family's income. He received average grades in school but was considered a hardworking and intelligent student with a curious bent of mind.

Kalam was the youngest of the five siblings, the eldest of whom was a sister, Asim Zohra, followed by three elder brothers—Mohammed Muthu Meera Lebbai Maraikayar, Mustafa Kamal and Kasim Mohammed. Kalam was extremely close to his siblings as well as their extended families throughout his life. He would regularly send small sums of money to his older relations but he himself remained a life-long bachelor.

Kalam's father wasn't educated, but he wanted Kalam to study. It is said that Kalam would get up at 4 am, bathe, and then go for his mathematics class. This particular teacher took only five students in the whole session; and bathing before the class was a condition he had laid to all his students. After his morning class, Kalam along with his cousin Samsuddin went around the town distributing

the newspaper. As the town had no electricity, kerosene lamps were lit. But as Kalam studied until 11, his mother would save some kerosene oil for him for later use.

Kalam always had the support of his school teachers as he was a promising student. Schwarzt High School's Iyadurai Solomon, who was a mentor and guide to Kalam, often told Kalam that if one truly, intensely desired something, there was no force in the world that would not let one achieve it. 'This made me fearless,' remarked Dr Kalam during one of his interviews later. Outside school, Ahmed Jallaluddin, who later became Kalam's brother-in-law, and Samsuddin, encouraged Kalam to appreciate nature's wonders. So at once, while growing up, he was exposed to a religious yet practical way of looking at the world.

During his school days, Kalam scored average grades. Nevertheless, he was described as a bright and hardworking student. He spent hours on his studies, especially mathematics. After completing his education at the Schwartz Higher Secondary School, Ramanathapuram, Kalam went on to attend Saint Joseph's College in Tiruchirappalli, then affiliated with the University of Madras. From there he graduated in physics in 1954.

Post his graduation from Tiruchirappalli, Kalam moved to Madras in 1955 to study aerospace engineering at the Madras Institute of Technology (MIT). This was an attempt at fulfilling his childhood ambition of becoming a fighter pilot. However, he narrowly missed achieving his dream. While Kalam was working on a senior class project, the Dean was dissatisfied with his lack of progress and threatened to cancel his scholarship unless the project was finished within the next three days. This made Kalam

work relentlessly on the project and he finally met the deadline, thus impressing the Dean. This incident left a deep impact on Kalam's psychology and taught him the value of time—a quality he imbibed for the rest of his life.

Kalam narrowly missed achieving his dream of becoming a fighter pilot, as he was placed in the ninth position among the qualifiers, and there were only eight positions available in Indian Air Force (IAF).

Kalam, from his younger days, was fascinated by the flight of birds. Years later, he realized that he wanted to fly aircraft. Although he took up Physics at St Joseph's College, Trichi, after schooling, towards the end, he was dissatisfied with his choice. When he discovered aeronautical engineering, he regretted having lost three precious years at the college.

Career as a Scientist

Kalam graduated from MIT in 1960, majoring in Aeronautical Engineering. He then took up the position of chief scientist at the Aeronautical Development Establishment of the Defence Research and Development Organisation (DRDO) as a scientist. One of his projects at DRDO was to design a small helicopter for the Indian Army but he remained skeptical of his choice of a job there. While at DRDO, he also got an opportunity to become a part of the Indian National Committee for Space Research (INCOSPAR) working under Vikram Sarabhai, the renowned space scientist.

In 1969, Kalam was transferred to the Indian Space Research Organisation (ISRO). As the Project Director, he was deeply involved in the development of India's first indigenous Satellite Launch Vehicle (SLV-III), which successfully deployed the Rohini satellite in near-Earth's orbit in July 1980. Kalam had first started work on an expandable rocket project independently at DRDO in 1965. In 1969, on receiving the government's approval, he expanded the programme to include more engineers.

One particular trait that endeared Kalam to people was that he never gave up even if he met with failure. He once said, 'I knew that for success, we have to work hard and persevere.' He drew strength from philosophy, religion and literature to win over his professional setbacks. With time, he also learnt to deal with professional jealousy and uncooperative team members.

In 1963–64, he visited NASA's Langley Research Centre in Hampton, Virginia; Goddard Space Flight Centre in Greenbelt, Maryland; and Wallops Flight Facility, Virginia. Between the 1970s and 1990s, Kalam made an effort to develop the Polar Satellite Launch Vehicle (PSLV) and SLV-III projects, both of which proved to be highly successful endeavours.

Kalam was invited by Raja Ramanna, the famous physicist best known for his role in India's nuclear programme during its early stages. He had called Kalam to witness the country's first nuclear test of Smiling Buddha as the representative of Terminal Ballistics Research Laboratory (TBRL), even though he had not participated in its development.

Although Kalam led several projects in his professional life, he treated each one like his last. Such was his passion. His advisor, Major General R. Swaminathan, explained Kalam's success as a leader in the following words: "He has this unique capability of being a boss as well as a worker. He can take on any role with ease."

In the 1970s, Kalam also directed two projects—Project Devil and Project Valiant—which sought to develop ballistic missiles from the technology of the successful SLV programme. Despite the displeasure of the Union Cabinet, Prime Minister Indira Gandhi allotted secret funds for

these aerospace projects through her discretionary powers under Kalam's directorship. Kalam also played a key role in convincing the Union Cabinet to cover up the true nature of these classified aerospace projects.

His research and educational leadership brought him great laurels and reputation in the 1980s. This encouraged the government to initiate an advanced missile programme under his directorship.

The then Defence Minister, R. Venkataraman, was involved in getting the cabinet approval for allocating Rs. 388 crore for the mission, named Integrated Guided

Missile Development Programme (IGMDP). He appointed Kalam as the chief executive of IGMDP. Kalam played a major role here as well. He developed many missiles under the mission including Agni, an intermediate range of ballistic missile, and Prithvi, the tactical surface-to-surface missile, although the projects faced much criticism for mismanagement, costs and time overruns.

Kalam served as the Chief Scientific Adviser to the Prime Minister as well as the Secretary of the Defence Research and Development Organisation from July 1992

to December 1999. He played a pivotal organizational, technical and political role in India's Pokhran-II nuclear test in 1998, the first since the original nuclear test by India in 1974. He also served as the Chief Project Coordinator, along with Rajagopala Chidambaram, during the testing phase of the nuclear test. Media coverage of Kalam during this period made him the country's best known nuclear scientist.

Kalam ensured that whatever technology was created by him was put to multiple use. One such example was the

light-weight carbon-compound material he designed for Agni. This he used to make calipers for people affected with polio. This carbon composite material reduced the weight of the calipers to 400 grams (from its original weight of 4 kg). Sometime later, addressing a conference at Athens, Greece, Kalam said, "Seeing the children run with lighter calipers brought tears to the eyes of their parents. That was the real moment of bliss for me."

In 2009, Kalam became the first Asian to be bestowed the Hoover Medal, America's top engineering prize, for his outstanding contribution to public service. The citation gave him recognition for making state-of-the-art healthcare available to the common man at affordable prices and bringing quality medical care to rural areas using spin-offs of defence technology.

Back home, Prithvi, Agni, Akash, Trishul and Nag missiles—all developed under the able guidance of Kalam—were huge successes. He was awarded the Padma Bhushan (1981), Padma Vibhushan (1990) and Bharat Ratna (1997) by the Government of India for his services to DRDO, ISRO, and to the Indian government. Kalam became the third President of India to have been honoured with a Bharat Ratna before being elected to the highest office, the other two being Sarvepalli Radhakrishnan and Zakir Husain. He was also the first scientist and first bachelor to occupy Rashtrapati Bhavan.

Kalam was also the Chancellor of Indian Institute of Space Science and Technology (Thiruvananthapuram),

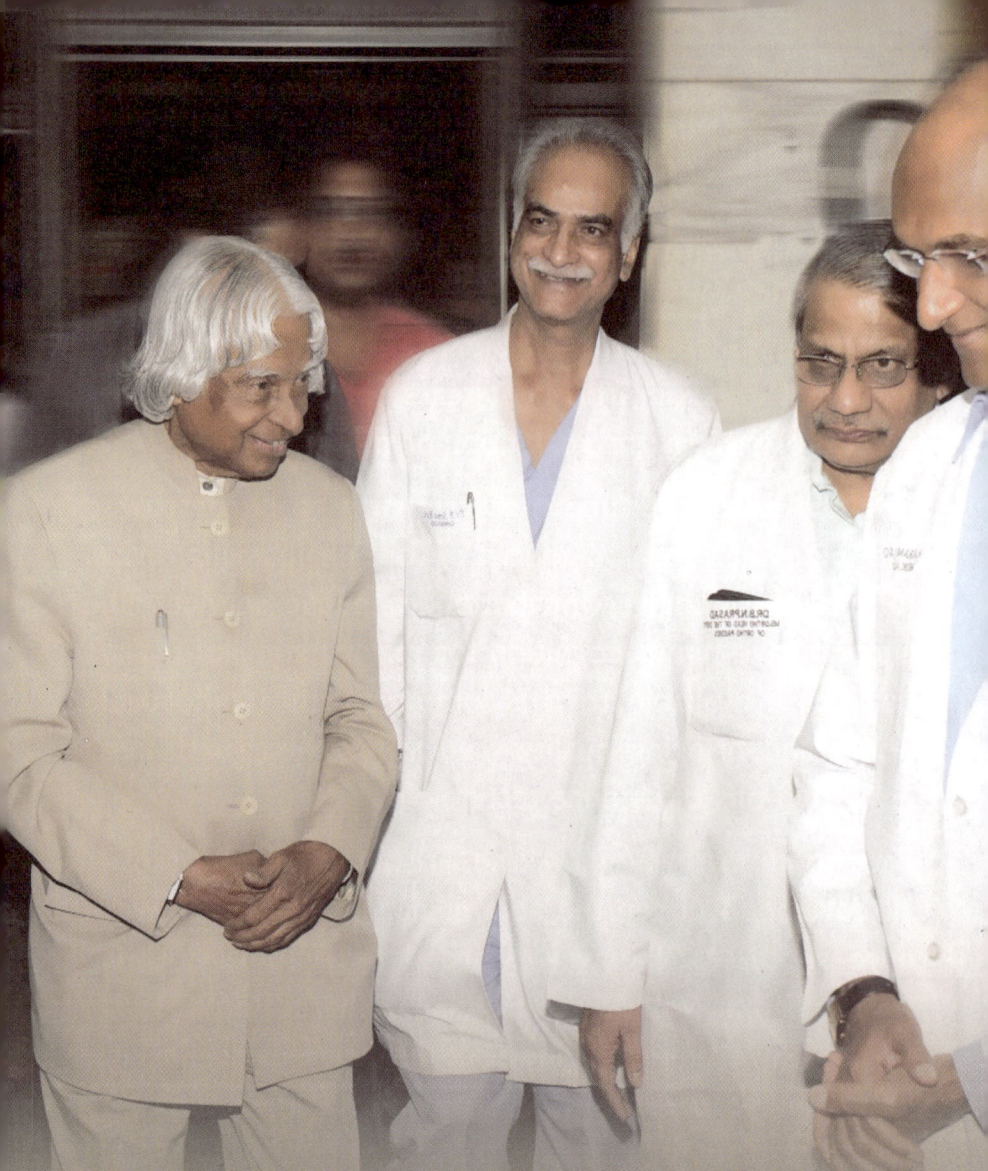

a professor at Anna University (Chennai) and adjunct/visiting faculty at many other academic and research institutions across India.

In 1998, along with cardiologist Soma Raju, Kalam developed a low-cost coronary stent, named the Kalam-Raju Stent. In 2012, the duo designed a rugged tablet computer for health care in rural areas, which was named the Kalam-Raju Tablet.

Journey and Achievements as a Scientist

- After completing his graduation in 1960, Kalam joined as a scientist in Defense Research and Development Organisation's Aeronautical Development Establishment.
- At the very start of his career he designed a small helicopter for the Indian Army.
- He worked under the famous scientist Vikram Sarabhai as a part of the committee of INCOSPAR.
- From 1963 to 1964, Kalam visited the Goddard Space Flight Center in Greenbelt, Maryland; the Wallops Flight Facility located at the Eastern Shore of Virginia; and the Langley Research Center of NASA, Virginia.
- In 1965, he started working independently in Defence Research and Development Organization on an expandable rocket project. The programme was expanded in 1969 and more engineers were included after receiving approval from the Indian government.
- He became the Project Director of India's first indigenous Satellite Launch Vehicle (SLV-III) when he was transferred to Indian Space Research Organisation in 1969. In the year 1980, his team was successful in deploying the Rohini satellite near the orbit of the Earth.

- Kalam's efforts in developing the projects on SLV-III and Polar SLV from 1970s to 1990s met with success.

- Kalam directed Project Valiant and Project Devil. These aimed at developing ballistic missiles using the same technology as used in the SLV programme that was a success. It is believed that the then prime minister, Indira Gandhi, used her discretionary powers and allotted secret funds when these aerospace projects were disapproved by the Union Cabinet.

- Kalam and Dr. V.S. Arunachalam, on the proposal of the then Defence Minister R. Venkataraman, worked on developing a quiver of missiles instead of one at a time. Kalam was chosen as the chief executive of the programme which was named Integrated Guided Missile Development Programme.

- From July 1992 to December 1999, Kalam remained the Secretary of the Defence Research and Development Organization and also the Chief Scientific Advisor to the prime minister. It was during this period that India witnessed the Pokhran II nuclear tests in which Kalam played a key technological and political role. At the time of the testing phase, he, along with R. Chidambaram, was made the chief project coordinator.

- Kalam was instrumental in developing a low-cost coronary stent along with Dr. Soma Raju, a cardiologist, in 1998. They are credited with designing a tablet PC called 'Kalam-Raju Tablet' for healthcare in rural areas.

Personal Life

Kalam was noted for his truthfulness and his simple way of living. So simple was his lifestyle that he never even owned a television. Every day, he would wake up at 7 in the morning and retire to bed by 2 a.m. He had few

personal possessions which included his books, his veena, some clothing, a CD player and a laptop. On his death, he left no will and his possessions went to his eldest brother who survived him.

Religion and spirituality held much importance to him and he remained a devoted man throughout his life. He was a proud and a practicing Muslim. He would offer namāz and fast during Ramadan. His father, being the imam of a mosque in his hometown of Rameswaram, had strictly instilled these Islamic customs from his

childhood. His father had also taught him to respect other faiths when he was a little boy. As Kalam recalled, "Every evening, my father, A.P. Jainulabdeen, an imam, Pakshi Lakshmana Sastry, the head priest of the Ramanathaswamy Hindu temple, and a church priest used to sit with hot tea and discuss the issues concerning the island. He often said, 'For great men, religion is a way of making friends; small people make religion a fighting tool.'"

In addition to his faith in the Koran and Islamic practices, Kalam was well-versed in Hindu traditions as well. He learnt Sanskrit, read the Bhagavad Gita and followed vegetarian food habits. He also enjoyed writing Tamil poetry, playing the veena and listened to Carnatic devotional music every day.

Leading the Country

Kalam served as the eleventh President of India. He succeeded K. R. Narayanan in the year 2002 after winning the presidential election with an electoral vote of 922,884, surpassing the 107,366 votes won by Lakshmi Sahgal, the other contestant. His term lasted from July 25, 2002 to July 25, 2007.

On June 10, 2002, the National Democratic Alliance (NDA), which was in power at the time, expressed that they would nominate Kalam for the post of president, and both the Samajwadi Party and the Nationalist Congress Party backed his candidacy. After the Samajwadi Party announced its support for Kalam, Narayanan chose not to seek a second term in office, leaving the field clear for other candidates. On June 18, Kalam filed his nomination papers in the Indian Parliament, accompanied by Vajpayee and his senior Cabinet colleagues. The polling for the presidential election began on July 15, 2002 in Parliament and the state assemblies. Eventually, Kalam became the eleventh president of the Republic of India in an easy

victory. He moved into the Rashtrapati Bhavan after he was sworn in on July 25, 2002.

Kalam was the third president of India to have been honoured with a Bharat Ratna, India's highest civilian honour, before becoming the president. Dr Sarvepalli Radhakrishnan (1954) and Dr Zakir Hussain (1963) were the earlier recipients of Bharat Ratna, who later became the presidents of the country. Kalam was also the first scientist and the first bachelor to occupy Rashtrapati Bhawan.

During his term as the president of the world's largest democracy—India—he was affectionately known as the

'People's President'. During his tenure, Kalam was severely criticised for his inaction in deciding the fate of 20 out of the 21 mercy petitions submitted to him during his tenure. Article 72 of the Constitution of India empowers the president of India to grant pardons, and suspend or commute the death sentence of convicts. However, Kalam acted on only one mercy plea in his five-year tenure as the president, rejecting the plea of the other 21 convicts.

Known as the People's President, Kalam set a goal of conducting 500,000 one-on-one meetings with the young people over the course of his five-year term. His immense popularity led to him being nominated by MTV for a Youth Icon of the Year award in 2003 and 2006.

Post-Presidency

After serving his term as president of India in 2007, Kalam became a visiting professor at the Indian Institute of Management, Shillong; the Indian Institute of Management, Ahmedabad; and the Indian Institute of Management, Indore. He was an honorary fellow of Indian Institute of Science, Bangalore; Chancellor of the Indian Institute of Space Science and Technology, Thiruvananthapuram;

professor of Aerospace Engineering, Anna University, and many other academic and research institutions across India.

In May 2012, Kalam launched a programme for the youth of India called the 'What Can I Give Movement,' with a central theme of defeating corruption.

Kalam took an active interest in other developments in the field of science and technology, including a research programme for developing biomedical implants. He had set a target of interacting with 100,000 students during the two years after his resignation from the post of scientific adviser in 1999. He once stated, "I feel comfortable in the company of young people, particularly high school students. Henceforth, I intend to share with them experiences helping them to ignite their imagination and preparing them to work for a developed India for which the road map is already available."

Final Parting

On July 27, 2015, Kalam travelled to Shillong to deliver a lecture on 'Creating a Livable Planet Earth' at the Indian Institute of Management, Shillong. At around 6:35 p.m. just five minutes after his lecture had begun, he collapsed. He was rushed to the nearby Bethany Hospital in a critical condition but could not be saved. On reaching there, he lacked a pulse or any other signs of life. His last words, to his aide Srijan Pal Singh, were reported to be, "Funny guy! Are you doing well?"

Kalam's body was airlifted in an Indian Air Force helicopter from Shillong to Guwahati from where it was flown to New Delhi on the morning of July 28, in an air force C-130J Hercules.

Kalam's death caused an outpouring of grief from the entire nation and the world at large. Numerous tributes were paid to the former president across the nation and on social media. The government declared a seven-day state mourning period as a mark of respect.

Mourning the loss of Kalam, Prime Minister Narendra Modi said, "His death is a great loss to the scientific community. He took India to great heights. He showed the way."

Kathleen Wynne, the Premier of Ontario, which Kalam had visited on numerous occasions, expressed, "Deepest condolences ... as a respected scientist, he played a critical role in the development of the Indian space programme.

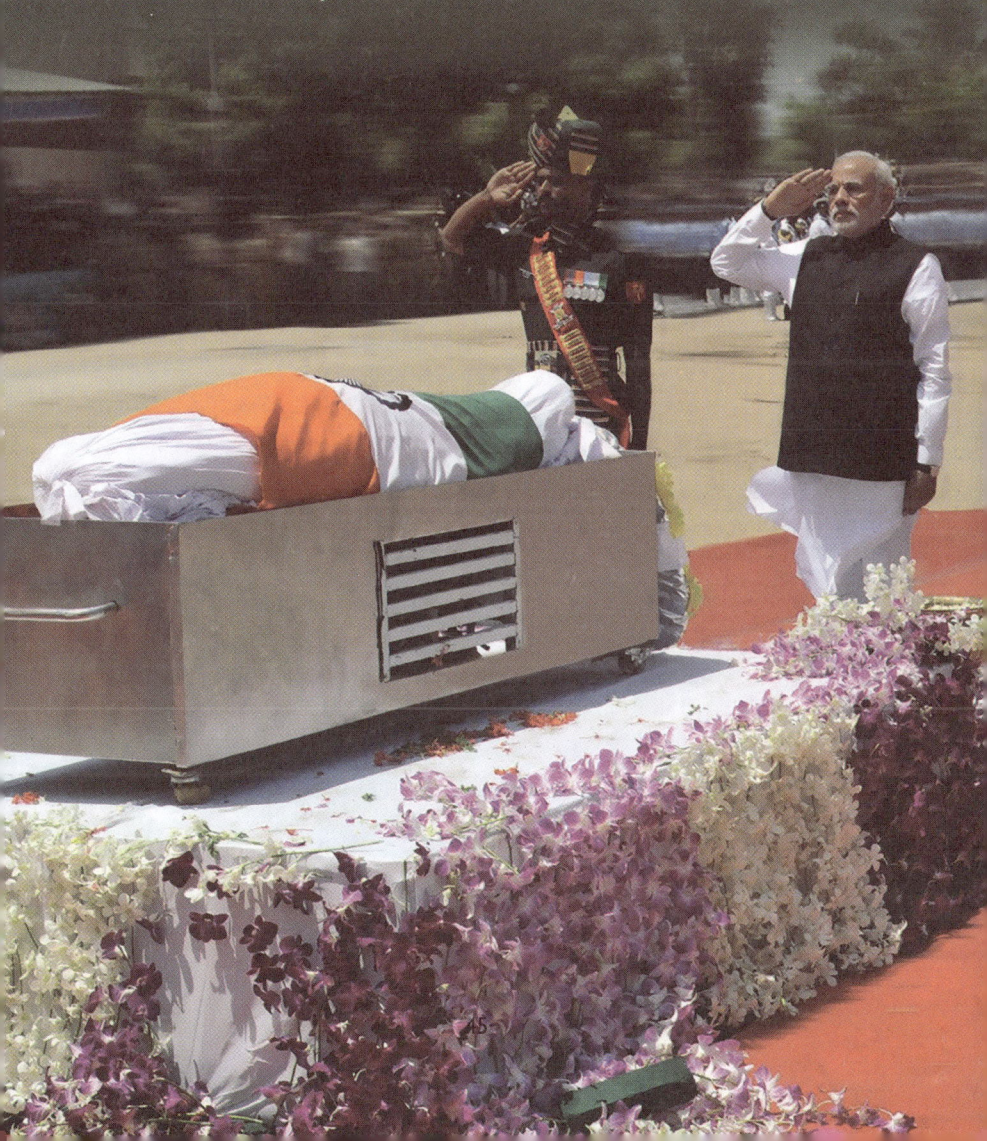

As a committed educator, he inspired millions of young people to achieve their very best. Also, as a devoted leader, he gained support both at home and abroad, becoming known as 'the people's President'. I join our Indo-Canadian families, friends, and neighbours in mourning the passing of this respected leader."

Barack Obama, the president of the United States stated, "Deepest condolences to the people of India on the passing of former Indian President Dr. A.P.J. Abdul Kalam."

This not only highlighted his achievements as a scientist and as a statesman, but also his role in strengthening U.S.–India relations and increasing space cooperation between the two nations.

Kalam, the Author

We get a glimpse of Kalam's bright, dazzling mind and his creativity through the many books that he had written. Some worth mention are Wings of Fire which is an autobiographical novel that tells the readers a story about unlocking their inner potential. In the book, Kalam strives to tell the reader the story of a boy (in this case himself) from a humble background who went on to become a key player in Indian space research/missile programmes and later became the president of India.

Another book by Kalam, which gained much acclaim from readers, is India 2020: A Vision for the New Millennium.

The book looks at the shortcomings and the qualities of India, as a country, and offers a dream of how India can develop to be among the world's initial four financial powers by 2020.

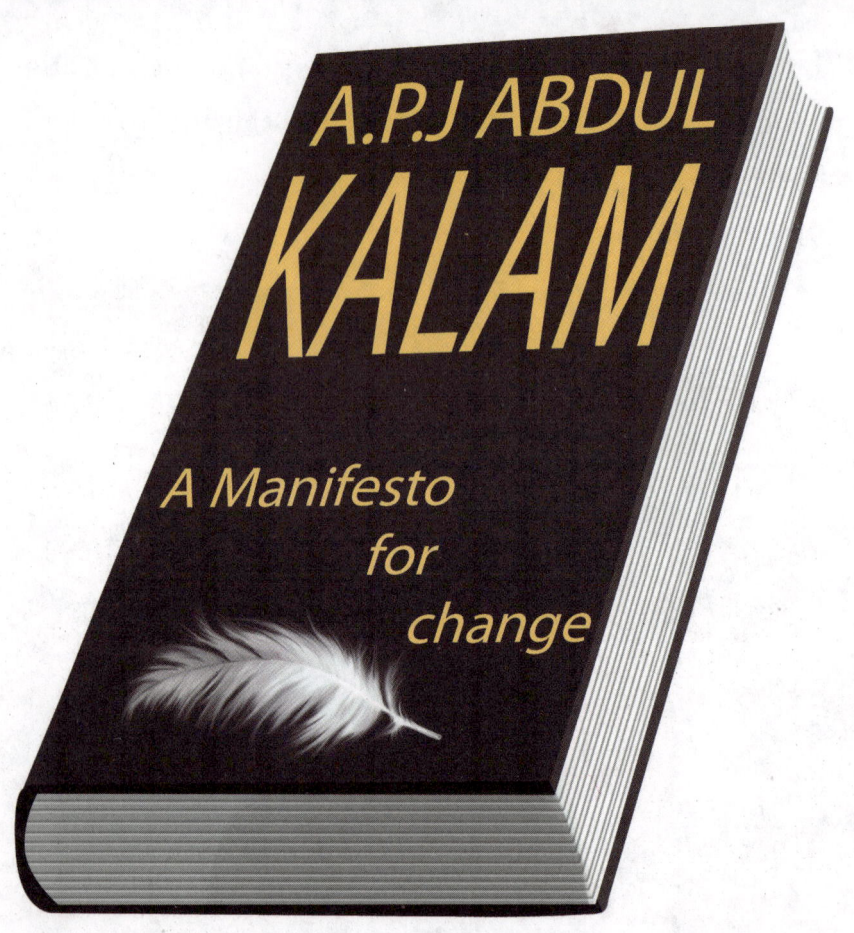

A Manifesto for Change, written by Kalam in collaboration with Y.S. Rajan, was a sequel to India 2020 published in 1998. The book, at that point in time, was considered surprisingly ahead of its times. In the book, Kalam shares his vision and dreams for a developed India. He emphasizes the importance of changes that Indians need to adopt in their governing methods. He has put together ideas for a better political leadership to bring about dramatic changes in India's growth and development. The book puts forth the authors' genuine aspirations and perspectives for a better, evolving nation and proposes that India could soon be one of the top five economies of the world.

Documentaries and Books by Dr. Kalam

- Ignited Minds: Unleashing the Power Within India
- Inspiring Thoughts
- Indomitable Spirit
- The Luminous Sparks
- Turning Points: A journey through challenges
- My Journey: Transforming Dreams into Actions

- Developments in Fluid Mechanics and Space Technology, by Dr. A.P.J. Abdul Kalam and Roddam Narasimha
- India 2020: A Vision for the New Millennium, by Dr. A.P.J. Abdul Kalam and Y.S. Rajan.
- Wings of Fire: An Autobiography, by Dr. A.P.J. Abdul Kalam and Arun Tiwari.
- Mission India, by Dr. A.P.J. Abdul Kalam .
- Envisioning an Empowered Nation, by Dr. A.P.J. Abdul Kalam and A. Sivathanu Pillai.
- You Are Born To Blossom: Take My Journey Beyond, by Dr. A.P.J. Abdul Kalam and Arun Tiwari.
- Target 3 Billion, by Dr. A.P.J. Abdul Kalam and Srijan Pal Singh

Biographies on Kalam:

A.P.J. Abdul Kalam: The Visionary of India, by K. Bhushan and G. Katyal.

Eternal Quest: Life and Times of Dr. Kalam, written by S. Chandra.

President A.P.J. Abdul Kalam, written by R.K. Pruthi.

My Days With Mahatma Abdul Kalam, written by Fr. A.K. George.

A Little Dream, a documentary film by P. Dhanapal, Minveli Media Works Private Limited.

The Kalam Effect: My Years with the President, written by P.M. Nair.

Awards and Accolades

Dr. Kalam was a person who taught, motivated and inspired millions across India and also the world. He has to his credit numerous awards and accolades. To mention first, he received honorary doctorates from 40 universities. The Government of India honoured him with the Padma Bhushan in 1981 and the Padma Vibhushan in 1990 for his work with ISRO and DRDO, and for his role as a scientific advisor to the government. In the year 1997, Kalam received India's highest civilian honour, the Bharat Ratna, for his contribution to the scientific research and modernisation of defence technology in India. He was

the recipient of the Von Braun Award from the National Space Society 'to recognize excellence in the management and leadership of a space-related project' in 2013.

After his death, Kalam received numerous tributes. The Tamil Nadu state government announced that his birthday, October 15, would be observed across the state as Youth Renaissance Day. The state government further announced the Dr. A.P.J. Abdul Kalam Award, constituting an 8 gram gold medal, a certificate and money. The award will be awarded annually on Independence Day, beginning in 2015, to residents of the state who have made significant achievements in promoting scientific growth, the humanities or the welfare of students.

Many educational and scientific institutions and other places were renamed and sometimes named in honour of this extraordinary man called Dr. Abdul Kalam.

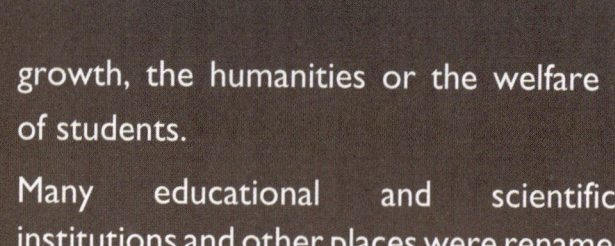

Timeline

- 1931   A.P.J. Abdul Kalam was born on October 15.

- 1954   He graduated from Saint Joseph's College, Tiruchirappalli.

- 1955   Kalam enrolled at the Madras Institute of Technology to study aerospace engineering.

- 1960   He joined Aeronautical Development Establishment of Defense Research and Development Organization (DRDO) as a chief scientist.

- 1969   He was transferred to the Indian Space Research Organization (ISRO).

- 1981   The Government of India honored Kalam with Padma Bhushan.

- 1990   Kalam was honored with Padma Vibhushan.

- 1992–1999   He served as the Chief Scientific Adviser to the prime minister and the secretary of Defence Research and Development Organisation.

- 1997   Kalam was honored with Bharat Ratna, India's highest civilian award.

Timeline

- 1997 He honoured with Indira Gandhi Award for National Integration.//
- 2002–2007 He served as the 11th President of India.
- 2015 He passed away on July 27, following a cardiac arrest.

Group Activity

Given below is a list of outstanding qualities of great human beings like Abdul Kalam. Weave a story highlighting one particular quality given to you by your teacher. Discuss in your group the plot, characters and situations to be portrayed in your story. Choose a suitable title for it too! Put down your story on a chart paper with appropriate pictures.

The qualities are:
- **Humility**
- **Perseverance**
- **Compassion**
- **Simplicity**
- **Passion**
- **Vision & Leadership**

Watching a Movie

The school authorities will arrange to show the movie *I Am Kalam* in their audio-visual room before the children read this biography.

Activities

Activities

Questions

1. Who was Abdul Kalam?
2. When and where was he born?
3. What was the tenure of his presidentship?
4. What was he popularly known as due to his work with ballistic missiles?
5. What did Kalam's parents do for their livelihood?
6. How many siblings did Kalam have?
7. Why did Kalam's family become poor when they were actually rich?
8. Name the school in which Kalam studied in his childhood.
9. What kind of a student was he?
10. From which institute did Kalam pass his aeronautical engineering?
11. What was his actual ambition and why did he not succeed in that?
12. After passing out of his engineering, where did Kalam join his first job?
13. What did he join as?

14. Name the two projects that Kalam directed in the year 1970.

15. In his personal life, what kind of a person was Kalam?

16. Why do you think Kalam was called the 'people's president'?

17. Why did Kalam say that he was very comfortable with young people?

18. Name a few books that Kalam had written.

19. When and how did Kalam die?

20. What is the best message you think he gave to us with his immense good work?

Activities

Glossary

achievement: something done successfully with effort

aeronautical engineering: the primary field of engineering concerned with the development of aircraft and spacecraft

affectionately: a way that shows fondness for someone

affiliated: officially attached with or connected to some organization

ancestral: belonging to or inherited from an ancestor

announced: to make a formal public statement about some truth

appreciate: to recognize the full worth of someone or something

autobiography: an account of a person's life written by that person himself

ballistic missiles: a missile with a high, arching trajectory, which is initially powered and guided but falls under gravity on to its target

biomedical implants: medical implants are man-made devices, in contrast to a transplant, which is a transplanted biomedical tissue; the surface of implants that contacts the body might be made of a biomedical material such as titanium, silicone, or apatite

cardiologist: a doctor who specializes in the study or treatment of heart diseases

colleagues: a person with whom one works

coronary stent: a tube-shaped device placed in the coronary arteries that supplies blood to the heart to keep the arteries open

corruption: dishonest or fraudulent conduct by people in power

deployed: to move troops or equipment into position for military action

dissatisfied: not content or happy with something

extraordinary: very unusual or remarkable

imam: a person who leads prayers in a mosque

impressing: to make someone feel admired

inaction: lack of any action

missile: an object which is propelled at a target by force from a mechanical weapon

pilgrim: a person who journeys to a sacred place for religious purposes

recipients: a person who receives an award

Glossary

renowned: known or talked about by many people

reputation: the beliefs or opinions that are generally held by all about someone or something

siblings: a brother or sister

skeptical: someone who is not easily convinced

spirituality: to do with religion and God

succeeding: coming after something in time

surpassing: incomparable

tactical: to plan actions carefully to gain a specific military end

transferred: to move from one place to another